Engineering Our World

How a House Is Built

By Theresa Emminizer

Gareth Stevens
PUBLISHING

Please visit our website, www.garethstevens.com. For a free color catalog of all our high-quality books, call toll free 1-800-542-2595 or fax 1-877-542-2596.

Library of Congress Cataloging-in-Publication Data

Names: Emminizer, Theresa, author.
Title: How a house is built / Theresa Emminizer.
Description: New York : Gareth Stevens Publishing, 2021. | Series: Engineering our world |
Includes index. | Contents: Home Sweet Home – Who Builds the House? – First, the Foundation –
Framing the House – Putting in the Inner Systems – Drywall, Trim, and Finishes – Exterior Work and
Landscaping – Everyday Wonders – Build Your Own House. |
Summary: "In this fun and informative text, readers will take an eye-opening look at home
construction, learning what houses are made of, who builds them, and how the process can be
broken down into steps"– Provided by publisher.
Identifiers: LCCN 2019027295 | ISBN 9781538247037 (paperback) | ISBN 9781538247044 | ISBN
9781538247051 (library binding) | ISBN 9781538247068 (ebook)
Subjects: LCSH: House construction–Juvenile literature.
Classification: LCC TH4811.5 .E46 2020 | DDC 690/.837–dc23
LC record available at https://lccn.loc.gov/2019027295

First Edition

Published in 2021 by
Gareth Stevens Publishing
111 East 14th Street, Suite 349
New York, NY 10003

Designer: Sarah Liddell
Editor: Monika Davies

Photo credits: Cover, p. 1 romakoma/Shutterstock.com; background Jason Winter/
Shutterstock.com; pp. 5, 19 Monkey Business Images/Shutterstock.com; p. 7 Sean Locke
Photography/Shutterstock.com; p. 9 Ivan_Sabo/Shutterstock.com; p. 11 Dave Tanner/
Shutterstock.com; p. 13 Arturs Budkevics/Shutterstock.com; p. 15 dotshock/Shutterstock.com;
p. 17 StockCube/Shutterstock.com; p. 20 (scissors) Kozak Sergii/Shutterstock.com; p. 20 (blue
pencil) Satori Studio/Shutterstock.com; p. 20 (cardboard) Michael_JayBerlin/Shutterstock.com;
p. 20 (ruler) QuangHo/Shutterstock.com; pp. 20, 21 (popsicle sticks) Thanwa photo/
Shutterstock.com; p. 21 (hot glue gun) Vadarshop/Shutterstock.com.

Printed in the United States of America

Some of the images in this book illustrate individuals who are models. The depictions do not imply actual
situations or events.

CPSIA compliance information: Batch #CS20GS: For further information contact Gareth Stevens, New York, New York at 1-800-542-2595.

Contents

Words in the glossary appear in **bold** type the first time they are used in the text.

Home Sweet Home

As the saying goes, home is where the heart is! Have you ever looked at a house and wondered how it was built? You might've also wondered who **designed** the house or how it was all put together.

From drawing up the plans to building the walls and putting on the finishing touches, a lot of work goes into making the places we call home. It's a lengthy **process** that takes a team of workers. Read on to discover how a house is built from start to finish!

Building Blocks

An architect is a person who designs a building. They create a **blueprint** that will guide the construction crew as they build the house.

DO YOU LIVE IN A HOUSE? ASK YOUR FAMILY IF YOU CAN FIND OUT WHEN AND HOW IT WAS BUILT.

Who Builds the House?

The main person in charge of building a house is the general contractor. When someone wants to build a house, they meet with a contractor to talk about the project and make a plan. The contractor will then hire a team of people to help do the work.

The contractor takes care of getting all of the supplies and gear that will be needed for construction. They also make a timeline for when each step will be completed.

Building Blocks

A surveyor is someone who prepares a location for construction. Surveyors take the measurements of the property and give the homeowner and contractor a report about the land.

CONTRACTORS ARE IN CHARGE OF KEEPING TRACK OF THE WHOLE BUILDING PROJECT AND OVERSEEING THE DAY-TO-DAY WORK OF BUILDING A HOUSE.

First, the Foundation

The first step to building a house is to prepare the site and build the **foundation.** This is the lowest level of the house.

The ground where the house will be built must be leveled, or evened out, and all the rocks and trees must also be cleared away. Once this is done, the crew digs a hole and builds footings. Footings are the **structures** made from **concrete** where the house touches the soil. If the house will have a basement, concrete is then poured to form the floors and walls.

Building Blocks

There are three main types of foundation: slab, crawl-space, and full basement. For slabs, after the footings are poured, the area between them is leveled and later filled with concrete to form a pad.

THE CONCRETE FOOTINGS AND FOUNDATION FOR A HOUSE MUST BE STRONG. THEY WILL SUPPORT, OR HOLD UP, THE WEIGHT OF THE WHOLE HOUSE.

Framing the House

Once the foundation is in place, the next step is to build the house's frame. The frame acts as the house's skeleton, or shell. It is the **framework** upon which the floors, walls, the inside tops of rooms, and roof of the home will later be built.

Once the frame is completed, it's covered in an outside layer called sheathing. The sheathing is then wrapped in house wrap. Both layers work together to keep water out. This stops the house's wooden frame from rotting.

Building Blocks

A house's roof is put on during the framing stage. This keeps the house's interior, or inside, safe from the weather outside. Builders can then work on the inside of the house.

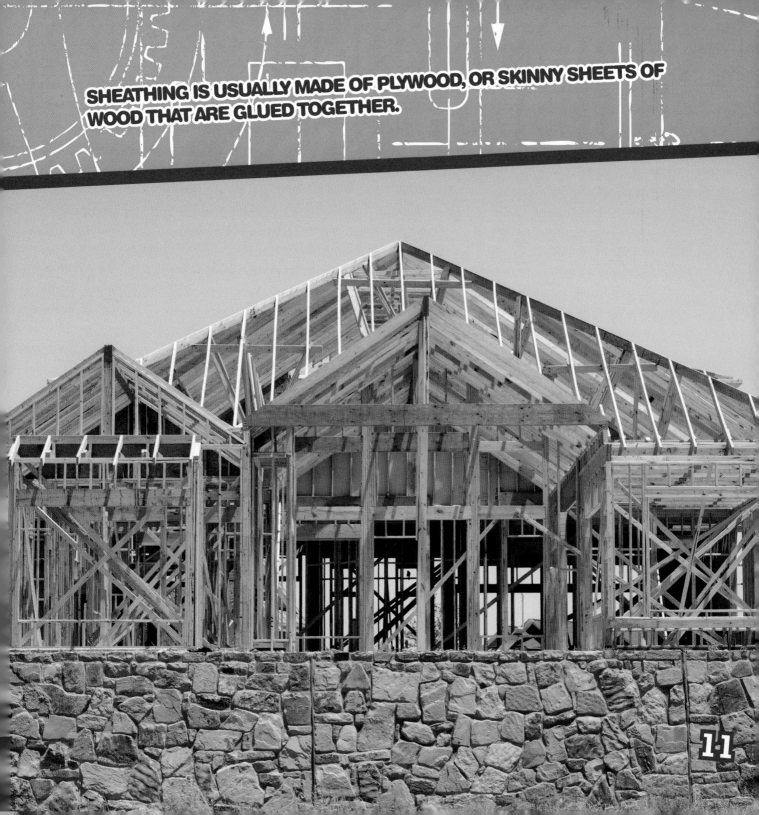

SHEATHING IS USUALLY MADE OF PLYWOOD, OR SKINNY SHEETS OF WOOD THAT ARE GLUED TOGETHER.

11

Putting in the Inner Systems

After the frame is completed, electricians and **plumbers** can begin work setting up the electrical and plumbing systems. These pipes and wires run through the walls, ceilings, and floors of the house. Setups are also put in for the HVAC system, which includes heating, ventilation (providing fresh air), and air-conditioning. This is called ductwork.

During this time, showers and bathtubs are also put in. Later, insulation is added into the walls. Insulation is the **material** used to keep a house warm and dry.

Building Blocks

As each step of the home-building process is completed, a home inspector checks to make sure everything was done properly. Inspectors are specially trained to make sure houses are safe.

PUTTING IN A HOUSE'S FIRST ELECTRICAL WIRES AND PLUMBING PIPES IS CALLED ROUGH WORK. THE REST OF THE WORK IS FINISHED AT A LATER STAGE IN THE BUILDING PROCESS.

13

Drywall, Trim, and Finishes

Next, drywall is put up. Drywall is a type of board that forms the interior walls and ceilings of houses. It's made of a combination of rock and paper. The seams, where the edges of the drywall meet, are then sealed together and smoothed out.

The house's trim, which includes interior doors, baseboards, and windowsills, is put in next. The walls can then be painted. The house's hard flooring, **cabinets**, and closets are also put in during this stage.

Building Blocks

Baseboards are the thin wooden boards that run along the bottom of interior walls. Windowsills are ledges, or thin, shelf-like surfaces, that hang off the bottom of windows.

FLOORS IN A HOUSE MAY BE MADE OF TILES, WOOD, OR VINYL. VINYL IS A TYPE OF PLASTIC.

Exterior Work and Landscaping

Once the interior of a house is finished, it's time to work on the exterior, or outside, of the house. This usually includes the driveway and any walkways or patios that might be added. Exterior work also includes landscaping. Landscaping is the process of designing the yard. Some homeowners choose to hire landscapers to plant trees and bushes to make their yards look pretty.

When all of the interior and exterior work is done, it's time to do a final "walk through" of the house.

A WALK THROUGH IS WHEN THE GENERAL CONTRACTOR AND HOMEOWNER TAKE ONE LAST LOOK AT THE FINISHED HOUSE TOGETHER.

17

Everyday Wonders

Though they may seem common, houses are actually wonderful feats of engineering! Engineering is the use of science and math to build better objects.

In house building, engineering is used to find answers to problems in each step of the process. Engineering is part of designing a house's layout, surveying the land, and constructing the building itself. Next time you look around your house, take a moment to value all of the work that went into making it a safe place for you to live!

Building Blocks

Building a house can take between 4 to 16 months. The length of time depends on where it's being built, how big it is, the time of year, and whether the house has special features.

THERE ARE MANY ELEMENTS TO CONSIDER WHEN BUILDING A HOUSE. THINK OF ALL OF THE ENGINEERING THAT WAS USED TO MAKE A PLACE FOR YOU TO LIVE!

Build Your Own House

Now that you know how a house is built, you can make your very own!

What You Need:

- paper

- blue colored pencil

- cardboard

- hot glue

- hot glue gun

- popsicle sticks

- ruler

- scissors

How to:

1. First, draw blueprints for your house! Use the paper and pencil to design what you'd like your house to look like.

2. Using your ruler and scissors, measure and cut pieces of cardboard for your house. One large piece will be your house's foundation, four smaller pieces will be your walls, and two pieces will be your roof.

3. On your cardboard foundation, measure and draw where your walls will go.

4. Your popsicle sticks will act as the frame of your house. Ask for an adult's help with your glue gun. Using hot glue, attach your popsicle sticks to the foundation.

5. Glue your four cardboard walls to the popsicle stick frame.

6. Glue the two pieces of cardboard to the top of the walls, making a roof.

7. Decorate your house!

Glossary

blueprint: the detailed plans or drawings that show how a building will be made

cabinet: a furniture piece that usually has shelves and is used for storing things, such as dishes in a kitchen

concrete: a mix of water, stones, sand, and a soft gray powder that becomes very hard and strong when it dries

design: to create the pattern or shape of something. Also, the pattern or shape of something.

foundation: a usually stone or concrete structure that holds up a building from the bottom

framework: a structure that holds up something

material: something used to make something

plumber: a worker who puts in or fixes sinks, toilets, water pipes, etc.

process: a series of steps or actions taken to complete something

structure: something built

For More Information

Books

Vonderman, Carol. *How to Be an Engineer*. New York, NY: DK Publishing, 2018.

McFadden, Jesse. *A Construction Worker's Tools*. New York, NY: PowerKids Press, 2016.

Morgan, Elizabeth. *Construction Workers*. New York, NY: PowerKids Press, 2016.

Websites

Building Big
www.pbs.org/wgbh/buildingbig/index.html
Learn about how larger structures, such as skyscrapers, are built.

e-GFI
students.egfi-k12.org
Are you interested in becoming an engineer? Find out more here!

How House Construction Works
home.howstuffworks.com/home-improvement/repair/house.htm
Take a closer look at the steps involved in building a house.

Index